INDIA

AN INTRO

SAMRAT PRATAP SINGH

This book has been dedicated to all the citizens of the great country India.

Contents

I

Introduction

India, officially the Republic of India (Hindi: Bhārat Gaṇarājya), is a country in South Asia. It is the seventh-largest country by area, the second-most populous country, and the most populous democracy in the world. Bounded by the Indian Ocean on the south, the Arabian Sea on the southwest, and the Bay of Bengal on the southeast, it shares land borders with Pakistan to the west; China, Nepal, and Bhutan to the north; and Bangladesh and Myanmar to the east. In the Indian Ocean, India is in the vicinity of Sri Lanka and the Maldives; its Andaman and Nicobar Islands share a maritime border with Thailand, Myanmar and Indonesia.

Modern humans arrived on the Indian subcontinent from Africa no later than 55,000 years ago. Their long occupation, initially in varying forms of isolation as hunter-gatherers, has made the region highly diverse, second only to Africa in human genetic diversity.Settled life emerged on the subcontinent in the western margins of the Indus river basin 9,000 years ago, evolving gradually into the Indus Valley Civilisation of the third millennium BCE. By 1200 BCE, an archaic form of Sanskrit, an Indo-European language, had diffused into India from the northwest, unfolding as the language of the Rigveda, and recording the dawning of Hinduism in India.The Dravidian languages of India were supplanted in the northern and western regions. By 400 BCE, stratification and exclusion by caste had emerged within Hinduism, and Buddhism and Jainism had arisen, proclaiming social orders unlinked to heredity.Early political consolidations gave rise to the loose-knit Maurya and Gupta Empires based in the Ganges Basin. Their collective era was suffused with wide-ranging creativity,but also marked by the declining status of women,and the incorporation of untouchability into an organised system of belief. In South India, the Middle kingdoms exported Dravidian-languages scripts and religious cultures to the kingdoms of Southeast Asia.

In the early medieval era, Christianity, Islam, Judaism, and Zoroastrianism put down roots on India's southern and western coasts. Muslim armies from Central Asia intermittently overran India's northern plains, eventually establishing the Delhi Sultanate, and drawing northern India into the cosmopolitan networks of medieval Islam. In the 15th century, the Vijayanagara Empire created a long-lasting composite Hindu culture in south India. In the Punjab, Sikhism emerged, rejecting institutionalised religion. The Mughal Empire, in 1526, ushered in two centuries of relative peace, leaving a legacy of luminous architecture.Gradually expanding rule of the British East India Company followed, turning India into a colonial economy, but also consolidating its sovereignty. British Crown rule began in 1858. The rights promised to Indians were granted slowly, but technological changes were introduced, and ideas of education, modernity and the public life took root. A pioneering and influential nationalist movement emerged, which was noted for nonviolent resistance and became the major factor in ending British rule. In 1947 the British Indian Empire was partitioned into two independent dominions, a Hindu-majority Dominion of India and a Muslim-majority Dominion of Pakistan, amid large-scale loss of life and an unprecedented migration.

India has been a federal republic since 1950, governed in a democratic parliamentary system. It is a pluralistic, multilingual and multi-ethnic society. India's population grew from 361 million in 1951 to 1.211 billion in 2011.During the same time, its nominal per capita income increased from US$64 annually to US$1,498, and its literacy rate from 16.6% to 74%. From being a comparatively destitute country in 1951, India has become a fast-growing major economy and a hub for information technology services, with an expanding middle class. It has a space programme which includes several planned or completed extraterrestrial missions. Indian movies, music, and spiritual teachings play an increasing role in global culture. India has substantially reduced its rate of poverty, though at the cost of increasing economic inequality. India is a nuclear-weapon state, which ranks high in military expenditure. It has disputes over Kashmir with its neighbours, Pakistan and China, unresolved since the mid-20th century. Among the socio-economic challenges India faces are gender inequality, child malnutrition, and rising levels of air pollution.India's land is megadiverse, with four biodiversity hotspots. Its forest cover comprises 21.7% of its area.India's wildlife, which has traditionally been viewed with tolerance in India's culture, is supported among these forests, and elsewhere, in protected habitats.

II

Etymology

According to the Oxford English Dictionary (third edition 2009), the name "India" is derived from the Classical Latin India, a reference to South Asia and an uncertain region to its east; and in turn derived successively from: Hellenistic Greek India (ʼΙνδία); ancient Greek Indos (ʼΙνδός); Old Persian Hindush, an eastern province of the Achaemenid empire; and ultimately its cognate, the Sanskrit Sindhu, or "river," specifically the Indus River and, by implication, its well-settled southern basin. The ancient Greeks referred to the Indians as Indoi (ʼΙνδοί), which translates as "The people of the Indus".

The term Bharat (Bhārat; pronounced [ˈbʱaːrət] , mentioned in both Indian epic poetry and the Constitution of India, is used in its variations by many Indian languages. A modern rendering of the historical name Bharatavarsha, which applied originally to North India,Bharat gained increased currency from the mid-19th century as a native name for India.

Hindustan ([ɦɪndʊˈstaːn] is a Middle Persian name for India, introduced during the Mughal Empire and used widely since. Its meaning has varied, referring to a region encompassing present-day northern India and Pakistan or to India in its near entirety

III

Geography

India accounts for the bulk of the Indian subcontinent, lying atop the Indian tectonic plate, a part of the Indo-Australian Plate. India's defining geological processes began 75 million years ago when the Indian Plate, then part of the southern supercontinent Gondwana, began a north-eastward drift caused by seafloor spreading to its south-west, and later, south and south-east. Simultaneously, the vast Tethyan oceanic crust, to its northeast, began to subduct under the Eurasian Plate.These dual processes, driven by convection in the Earth's mantle, both created the Indian Ocean and caused the Indian continental crust eventually to under-thrust Eurasia and to uplift the Himalayas. Immediately south of the emerging Himalayas, plate movement created a vast trough that rapidly filled with river-borne sediment and now constitutes the Indo-Gangetic Plain. Cut off from the plain by the ancient Aravalli Range lies the Thar Desert.

The Tungabhadra, with rocky outcrops, flows into the peninsular Krishna river.

Fishing boats lashed together before a monsoon storm in a tidal creek in Anjarle village, Maharashtra.

The original Indian Plate survives as peninsular India, the oldest and geologically most stable part of India. It extends as far north as the Satpura and Vindhya ranges in central India. These parallel chains run from the Arabian Sea coast in Gujarat in the west to the coal-rich Chota Nagpur Plateau in Jharkhand in the east.[167] To the south, the remaining peninsular landmass, the Deccan Plateau, is flanked on the west and east by coastal ranges known as the Western and Eastern Ghats;[168] the plateau contains the country's oldest rock formations, some over one billion years old. Constituted in such fashion, India lies to the north of the equator between 6° 44′ and 35° 30′ north latitude[i] and 68° 7′ and 97° 25′ east longitude.

India's coastline measures 7,517 kilometres (4,700 mi) in length; of this distance, 5,423 kilometres (3,400 mi) belong to peninsular India and 2,094 kilometres (1,300 mi) to the Andaman, Nicobar, and Lakshadweep island chains. According to the Indian naval hydrographic charts, the mainland coastline consists of the following: 43% sandy beaches; 11% rocky shores, including cliffs; and 46% mudflats or marshy shores.

Major Himalayan-origin rivers that substantially flow through India include the Ganges and the Brahmaputra, both of which drain into the Bay of Bengal. Important tributaries of the Ganges include the Yamuna and the Kosi; the latter's extremely low gradient, caused by long-term silt deposition, leads to severe floods and course changes.Major peninsular rivers, whose steeper gradients prevent their waters from flooding, include the Godavari, the Mahanadi, the Kaveri, and the Krishna, which also drain into the Bay of Bengal;and the Narmada and the Tapti, which drain into the Arabian Sea. Coastal features include the marshy Rann of Kutch of western India and the alluvial Sundarbans delta of eastern India; the latter is shared with Bangladesh. India has two archipelagos: the Lakshadweep, coral atolls off India's south-western coast; and the Andaman and Nicobar Islands, a volcanic chain in the Andaman Sea.

Indian climate is strongly influenced by the Himalayas and the Thar Desert, both of which drive the economically and culturally pivotal summer and winter monsoons. The Himalayas prevent cold Central Asian katabatic winds from blowing in, keeping the bulk of the Indian subcontinent warmer than most locations at similar latitudes.The Thar Desert plays a crucial role in attracting the moisture-laden south-west summer monsoon winds that, between June and October, provide the majority of India's rainfall. Four major climatic groupings predominate in India: tropical wet, tropical dry, subtropical humid, and montane.

Temperatures in India have risen by 0.7 °C (1.3 °F) between 1901 and 2018. Climate change in India is often thought to be the cause. The retreat of Himalayan glaciers has adversely affected the flow rate of the major Himalayan rivers, including the Ganges and the Brahmaputra. According to some current projections, the number and severity of droughts in India will have markedly increased by the end of the present century.

Set apart from the rest of Asia by the supreme continental wall of the Himalayas, the Indian subcontinent touches three large bodies of water and is immediately recognizable on any world map. It is the huge, terrestrial beak between Africa and Indonesia. This thick, roughly triangular peninsula defines the Bay of Bengal to the east, the Arabian sea to the west, and the India Ocean to the south.

India's puzzleboard of 26 states holds virtually every kind of landscape imaginable. An abundance of mountain ranges and national parks provide ample opportunity for eco-tourism and trekking, and its sheer size promises something for everyone. From its northernmost point on the Chinese border, India extends a good 2000 miles (3200 km) to its southern tip, where the island nation of Sri Lanka seems to be squeezed out of India like a great tear, the synapse forming the Gulf of Mannar. India's northern border is dominated mostly by Nepal and the Himalayas, the world's highest mountain chain. Following the sweeping mountains to the northeast, its borders narrow to a small channel that passes between Nepal, Tibet, Bangladesh, and Bhutan, then spreads out again to meet Burma in area called the "eastern triangle." Apart from the Arabian sea, its western border is defined exclusively by Pakistan.

India can be organized along the compass points. North India, shaped like a throat and two lungs, is the country's largest region.

It begins with the panhandle of Jammu and Kashmir, a dynamic area with terrain varying from arid mountains in the far north to the lake country and forests near Sringar and Jammu. Falling south along the Indus river valley, the North becomes flatter and more hospitable, widening into the fertile plains of Punjab to the west and the Himalayan foothills of Uttar Pradesh and the Ganges river valley to the East. Cramped between these two states is the capital city, Delhi. The southwestern extremity of the North is the large state of Rajastan, whose principal features are the Thar Desert and the stunning "pink city" of Jaipur. To the southeast is southern Uttar Pradesh and Agra, home of the famous Taj Mahal.

West India contains the states of Gujarat, Maharashtra, Goa, and part of the massive, central state of Madhya Pradesh. The west coast extends from the Gujarat peninsula down to Goa, and it is lined with some of India's best beaches. The land along the coast is typically lush, with rainforests reaching southward from Bombay all the way to into Goa. A long mountain chain, the Western Ghats, separates the verdant coast from the Vindya mountains and the dry Deccan plateau further inland.

Home of the sacred Ganges river and the majority of Himalayan foothills, East India begins with the states of Madhya Pradesh, Bihar, Orissa, which comprise the westernmost part of the region. East India also contains an area known as the eastern triangle, which is entirely distinct. This is the last gulp of land that extends beyond Bangladesh, culminating in the Naga Hills along the Burmese border.

India reaches its peninsular tip with South India, which begins with the Deccan in the north and ends with Cape Comorin, where Hindus believe that bathing in the waters of the three oceans will wash away their sins. The states in South India are Karnataka, Andhra Pradesh, Tamil Nadu, and Kerala, a favorite leisure destination. The southeast coast, mirroring the west, also rests snugly beneath a mountain range---the Eastern Ghats.

Because of India's size, its climate depends not only on the time of year, but also the location. In general, temperatures tend to be cooler in the north, especially between September and March. The south is coolest between November to January. In June, winds and warm surface currents begin to move northwards and westwards, heading out of the Indian Ocean and into the Arabian Gulf. This creates a phenomenon known as the south-west monsoon, and it brings heavy rains to the west coast. Between October and December, a similar climatic pattern called the north-east monsoon appears in the Bay of Bengal, bringing rains to the east coast. In addition to the two monsoons, there are two other seasons, spring and autumn.

Though the word "monsoon" often brings to mind images of torrential floods and landslides, the monsoon seasons are not bad times to come to India. Though it rains nearly every day, the downpour tends to come and go quickly, leaving behind a clean, glistening landscape.

IV

Divisions

India is a federal union comprising 28 states and 8 union territories (listed below as 1–28 and A–H, respectively). All states, as well as the union territories of Jammu and Kashmir, Puducherry and the National Capital Territory of Delhi, have elected legislatures and governments following the Westminster system of governance. The remaining five union territories are directly ruled by the central government through appointed administrators. In 1956, under the States Reorganisation Act, states were reorganised on a linguistic basis. There are over a quarter of a million local government bodies at city, town, block, district and village levels.

Andhra Pradesh
Arunachal Pradesh
Assam
Bihar
Chhattisgarh
Goa
Gujarat
Haryana
Himachal Pradesh
Jharkhand
Karnataka
Kerala

Madhya Pradesh
Maharashtra
Manipur
Meghalaya
Mizoram
Nagaland
Odisha
Punjab
Rajasthan
Sikkim
Tamil Nadu
Telangana
Tripura
Uttar Pradesh
Uttarakhand
West Bengal
Andaman and Nicobar Islands
Chandigarh
Dadra and Nagar Haveli and Daman and Diu
Jammu and Kashmir
Ladakh
Lakshadweep
National Capital Territory of Delhi
Puducherry

V

Culture and People

With nearly 1 billion citizens, India is the second most populous nation in the world. It is impossible to speak of any one Indian culture, although there are deep cultural continuities that tie its people together. English is the major language of trade and politics, but there are fourteen official languages in all. There are twenty-four languages that are spoken by a million people or more, and countless other dialects. India has seven major religions and many minor ones, six main ethnic groups, and countless holidays.

Religion is central to Indian culture, and its practice can be seen in virtually every aspect of life in the country. Hinduism is the dominant faith of India, serving about 80 percent of the population. Ten percent worship Islam, and 5 perscent are Sikhs and Christians; the rest (a good 45 million) are Buddhists, Jains, Bahai, and more.

VI

Economy

India has one of the largest, most highly diversified economies in the world, but, because of its enormous population, it is—in terms of income and gross national product (GNP) per capita—one of the poorest countries on Earth. Since independence, India has promoted a mixed economic system in which the government, constitutionally defined as "socialist," plays a major role as central planner, regulator, investor, manager, and producer. Starting in 1951, the government based its economic planning on a series of five-year plans influenced by the Soviet model. Initially, the attempt was to boost the domestic savings rate, which more than doubled in the half century following the First Five-Year Plan (1951–55). With the Second Five-Year Plan (1956–61), the focus began to shift to import-substituting industrialization, with an emphasis on capital goods. A broad and diversified industrial base developed. However, with the collapse of the Soviet system in the early 1990s, India adopted a series of free-market reforms that fueled the growth of its middle class, and its highly educated and well-trained workforce made India one of the global centres of the high-technology boom that began in the late 20th century and produced significant annual growth rates. The agricultural sector remains the country's main employer (about half of the workforce), though, with about one-fifth of the gross domestic product (GDP), it is no longer the largest contributor to GDP. Manufacturing remains another solid component of GDP. However, the major growth has been in trade, finance, and other services, which, collectively, are by far the largest component of GDP.

Many of the government's decisions are highly political, especially its attempts to invest equitably among the various states of the union. Despite the government's pervasive economic role, large corporate undertakings dominate many spheres of modern economic activity, while tens of millions of generally small agricultural holdings and petty commercial, service, and craft enterprises account for the great bulk of employment. The range of technology runs the gamut from the most traditional to the most sophisticated.

There are few things that India cannot produce, though much of what it does manufacture would not be economically competitive without the protection offered by tariffs on imported goods, which have remained high despite liberalization. In absolute terms and in relation to GDP, foreign trade traditionally has been low. Despite continued government regulation (which has remained strong in many sectors), trade expanded greatly beginning in the 1990s.

Probably no more than one-fifth of India's vast labour force is employed in the so-called "organized" sector of the economy (e.g., mining, plantation agriculture, factory industry, utilities, and modern transportation, commercial, and service enterprises), but that small fraction generates a disproportionate share of GDP, supports most of the middle- and upper-class population, and generates most of the economic growth. It is the organized sector to which most government regulatory activity applies and in which trade unions, chambers of commerce, professional associations, and other institutions of modern capitalist economies play a significant role. Apart from rank-and-file labourers, the organized sector engages most of India's professionals and virtually all of its vast pool of scientists and technicians.

VII

Government and society

The architects of India's constitution, though drawing on many external sources, were most heavily influenced by the British model of parliamentary democracy. In addition, a number of principles were adopted from the Constitution of the United States of America, including the separation of powers among the major branches of government, the establishment of a supreme court, and the adoption, albeit in modified form, of a federal structure (a constitutional division of power between the union [central] and state governments). The mechanical details for running the central government, however, were largely carried over from the Government of India Act of 1935, passed by the British Parliament, which served as India's constitution in the waning days of British colonial rule.

The new constitution promulgated on January 26, 1950, proclaimed India "a sovereign socialist secular democratic republic." With 395 articles, 10 (later 12) schedules (each clarifying and expanding upon a number of articles), and more than 90 amendments, it is one of the longest and most detailed constitutions in the world. The constitution includes a detailed list of "fundamental rights," a lengthy list of "directive principles of state policy" (goals that the state is obligated to promote, though with no specified timetable for their accomplishment [an idea taken from the Irish constitution]), and a much shorter list of "fundamental duties" of the citizen.

The remainder of the constitution outlines in great detail the structure, powers, and manner of operation of the union (central) and state governments. It also includes provisions for protecting the rights and promoting the interests of certain classes of citizens (e.g., disadvantaged social groups, officially designated as "Scheduled Castes" and "Scheduled Tribes") and the process for constitutional amendment. The extraordinary specificity of India's constitution is such that amendments, which average nearly two per year, have frequently been required to deal with issues that in other countries would be handled by routine legislation. With a few exceptions, the passage of an amendment requires only a simple majority of both houses of parliament, but this majority must form two-thirds of those present and voting.

Constitutional structure

The three lists contained in the constitution's seventh schedule detail the areas in which the union and state governments may legislate. The union list outlines the areas in which the union government has exclusive authority, which include foreign policy, defense, communications, currency, taxation on corporations and nonagricultural income, and railroads. State governments have the sole power to legislate on such subjects as law and order, public health and sanitation, local government, betting and gambling, and taxation on agricultural income, entertainment, and alcoholic beverages. The items on the concurrent list include those on which both the union government and state governments may legislate, though a union law generally takes precedence; among these areas are criminal law, marriage and divorce, contracts, economic and social planning, population control and family planning, trade unions, social security, and education. Matters requiring legislation that are not specifically covered in the listed powers lie within the exclusive domain of the central government.

An exceedingly important power of the union government is that of creating new states, combining states, changing state boundaries, and terminating a state's existence. The union government may also create and dissolve any of the union territories, whose powers are more limited than those of the states. Although the states exercise either sole or joint control over a substantial range of issues, the constitution establishes a more dominant role for the union government.

Union government

The three branches of the union government are charged with different responsibilities, but the constitution also provides a fair degree of interdependence. The executive branch consists of the president, vice president, and a Council of Ministers, led by the prime minister. Within the legislative branch are the two houses of parliament—the lower house, or Lok Sabha (House of the People), and the upper house, or Rajya Sabha (Council of States). The president of India is also considered part of parliament. At the apex of the judicial branch is the Supreme Court, whose decisions are binding on the higher and lower courts of the state governments.

Executive branch

India's head of state is the president who is elected to a five-year renewable term by an electoral college consisting of the elected members of both houses of parliament and the elected members of the legislative assemblies of all the states. The vice president, chosen by an electoral college made up of only the two houses of parliament, presides over the Rajya Sabha. If the president dies or otherwise leaves office, the vice president assumes the position until an election can be held.

The powers of the president are largely nominal and ceremonial, except in times of emergency, and the president normally acts on the advice of the prime minister. The proper limits of the president's power are sometimes a matter for debate. The president may, however, proclaim a national state of emergency when there is perceived to be a grave threat to the country's security or impose direct presidential rule at the state level when it is thought that a particular state legislative assembly has become incapable of functioning effectively. The president may also dissolve the Lok Sabha and call for new parliamentary elections after a prime minister loses a vote of confidence.

Effective executive power rests with the Council of Ministers, headed by the prime minister, who is chosen by the majority party or coalition in the Lok Sabha and is formally appointed by the president. The Council of Ministers, also formally appointed by the president, is selected by the prime minister. The most important group within the council is the cabinet. Cabinet portfolios are assigned partly on the basis of interest and competence but also on the basis of demonstrated loyalty to the ruling party or party leader and on the implicit need to represent the country's major regions and population groups (e.g., based on religion, language, caste, and gender). The prime minister and the Council of Ministers remain in power throughout the term of the Lok Sabha, unless they lose a vote of confidence.

Legislative branch

Of the two houses of parliament, the more powerful is the Lok Sabha, in which the prime minister leads the ruling party or coalition. The constitution limits the number of elected members of the Lok Sabha to 530 from the states and 20 from the union territories, allotted roughly in proportion to their population. The president may also nominate two members of the Anglo-Indian community if it appears that this community is not being adequately represented. Members of the Lok Sabha serve for terms of five years, unless the house is dissolved before that.

Membership in the Rajya Sabha is not to exceed 250. Of these members, 12 are nominated by the president to represent literature, science, art, and social service, and the balance are proportionally elected by the state legislative assemblies. The Rajya Sabha is not subject to dissolution, but one-third of its members retire at the end of every second year. Legislative bills may originate in either house—except for financial bills, which may originate only in the Lok Sabha—and require passage by simple majorities in both houses in order to become law.

Bureaucracy

The day-to-day functioning of the government is performed by permanent ministries and other public service agencies. These are led by members of the Indian Administrative Service and other specialized services, who are chosen by competitive examination. Rules of recruitment and retirement and conditions of service are determined by the Union Public Service Commission (or, for state governments, by state public service commissions). There has been a steady proliferation of agencies and growth in the size of the bureaucracy since independence, with a concomitant increase in regulations, which often impede—rather than facilitate—administration.

VIII
Cultural Life

India is a large and diverse polyglot nation whose tempo of life varies from region to region and from community to community. By the early 21st century the lifestyle of middle-class and affluent urban families differed little from that of urbanites in Europe, East Asia, or the Americas. For the most part, however, the flow of rural life continued much as it always had. Many small villages remained isolated from most forms of media and communications, and work was largely done by hand or by the use of animal power. Traditional forms of work and recreation only slowly have given way to habits and pastimes imported from the outside world. The pace of globalization was slow in much of rural India, and even in urban areas Western tastes in food, dress, and entertainment were adopted with discrimination. Indian fashions have remained the norm; Indians have continued to prefer traditional cuisine to Western fare; and, though Indian youths are as obsessed as those in the West with pop culture, Indians produce their own films and music (albeit, strongly influenced by Western styles), which have been extremely popular domestically and have been successfully marketed abroad.

Throughout India, custom and religious ritual are still widely observed and practiced. Among Hindus, religious and social custom follows the samskara, a series of personal sacraments and rites conducted at various stages throughout life. Observant members of other confessional communities follow their own rites and rituals. Among all groups, caste protocols have continued to play a role in enforcing norms and values, despite decades of state legislation to alleviate caste bias.

Daily life and social customs

Family and kinship

For almost all Indians the family is the most important social unit. There is a strong preference for extended families, consisting of two or more married couples (often of more than a single generation), who share finances and a common kitchen. Marriage is virtually universal, divorce rare, and virtually every marriage produces children. Almost all marriages are arranged by family elders on the basis of caste, degree of consanguinity, economic status, education (if any), and astrology. A bride traditionally moves to her husband's house. However, nonarranged "love marriages" are increasingly common in cities.

Within families, there is a clear order of social precedence and influence based on gender, age, and, in the case of a woman, the number of her male children. The senior male of the household—whether father, grandfather, or uncle—typically is the recognized family head, and his wife is the person who regulates the tasks assigned to female family members. Males enjoy higher status than females; boys are often pampered while girls are relatively neglected. This is reflected in significantly different rates of mortality and morbidity between the sexes, allegedly (though reliable statistics are lacking) in occasional female infanticide, and increasingly in the abortion of female fetuses following prenatal gender testing. This pattern of preference is largely connected to the institution of dowry, since the family's obligation to provide a suitable dowry to the bride's new family represents a major financial liability. Traditionally, women were expected to treat their husbands as if they were gods, and obedience of wives to husbands has remained a strong social norm. This expectation of devotion may follow a husband to the grave; within some caste groups, widows are not allowed to remarry even if they are bereaved at a young age.

Hindu marriage has traditionally been viewed as the "gift of a maiden" (kanyadan) from the bride's father to the household of the groom. This gift is also accompanied by a dowry, which generally consists of items suitable to start a young couple in married life. In some cases, however, dowries demanded by grooms and their families have become quite extravagant, and some families appear to regard them as means of enrichment. There are instances, a few of which have been highly publicized, wherein young brides have been treated abusively—even tortured and murdered—in an effort to extract more wealth from the bride's father. The "dowry deaths" of such young women have contributed to a reaction against the dowry in some modern urban families.

A Muslim marriage is considered to be a contractual relationship—contracted by the bride's father or guardian—and, though there are often dowries, there is formal reciprocity, in which the groom promises a mahr, a commitment to provide his bride with wealth in her lifetime.

Beyond the family the most important unit is the caste. Within a village all members of a single caste recognize a fictive kinship relation and a sense of mutual obligation, but ideas of fictive kinship extend also to the village as a whole. Thus, for example, a woman who marries and goes to another village never ceases to be regarded as a daughter of her village. If she is badly treated in her husband's village, it may become a matter of collective concern for her natal village, not merely for those of her own caste.

Festivals and holidays

Virtually all regions of India have their distinctive places of pilgrimage, local saints and folk heroes, religious festivals, and associated fairs. There are also innumerable festivals associated with individual villages or temples or with specific castes and cults. The most popular of the religious festivals celebrated over the greater part of India are Vasantpanchami (generally in February, the exact date determined by the Hindu lunar calendar), in honour of Sarasvati, the goddess of learning; Holi (February–March), a time when traditional hierarchical relationships are forgotten and celebrants throw coloured water and powder at one another; Dussehra (September–October), when the story of the Ramayana is reenacted; and Diwali (Divali; October–November), a time for lighting lamps and exchanging gifts. The major secular holidays are Independence Day (August 15) and Republic Day (January 26).

IX

History

The Indian subcontinent, the great landmass of South Asia, is the home of one of the world's oldest and most influential civilizations. In this article, the subcontinent, which for historical purposes is usually called simply "India," is understood to comprise the areas of not only the present-day Republic of India but also the republics of Pakistan (partitioned from India in 1947) and Bangladesh (which formed the eastern part of Pakistan until its independence in 1971). For the histories of these latter two countries since their creation, see Pakistan and Bangladesh.

Since early times the Indian subcontinent appears to have provided an attractive habitat for human occupation. Toward the south it is effectively sheltered by wide expanses of ocean, which tended to isolate it culturally in ancient times, while to the north it is protected by the massive ranges of the Himalayas, which also sheltered it from the Arctic winds and the air currents of Central Asia. Only in the northwest and northeast is there easier access by land, and it was through those two sectors that most of the early contacts with the outside world took place.

Within the framework of hills and mountains represented by the Indo-Iranian borderlands on the west, the Indo-Myanmar borderlands in the east, and the Himalayas to the north, the subcontinent may in broadest terms be divided into two major divisions: in the north, the basins of the Indus and Ganges (Ganga) rivers (the Indo-Gangetic Plain) and, to the south, the block of Archean rocks that forms the Deccan plateau region. The expansive alluvial plain of the river basins provided the environment and focus for the rise of two great phases of city life: the civilization of the Indus valley, known as the Indus civilization, during the 3rd millennium BCE; and, during the 1st millennium BCE, that of the Ganges. To the south of this zone, and separating it from the peninsula proper, is a belt of hills and forests, running generally from west to east and to this day largely inhabited by tribal people. This belt has played mainly a negative role throughout Indian history in that it remained relatively thinly populated and did not form the focal point of any of the principal regional cultural developments of South Asia. However, it is traversed by various routes linking the more-attractive areas north and south of it. The Narmada (Narbada) River flows through this belt toward the west, mostly along the Vindhya Range, which has long been regarded as the symbolic boundary between northern and southern India.

The northern parts of India represent a series of contrasting regions, each with its own distinctive cultural history and its own distinctive population. In the northwest the valleys of the Baluchistan uplands (now largely in Balochistan, Pakistan) are a low-rainfall area, producing mainly wheat and barley and having a low density of population. Its residents, mainly tribal people, are in many respects closely akin to their Iranian neighbours. The adjacent Indus plains are also an area of extremely low rainfall, but the annual flooding of the river in ancient times and the exploitation of its waters by canal irrigation in the modern period have enhanced agricultural productivity, and the population is correspondingly denser than that of Baluchistan. The Indus valley may be divided into three parts: in the north are the plains of the five tributary rivers of the Punjab (Persian: Panjāb, "Five Waters"); in the centre the consolidated waters of the Indus and its tributaries flow through the alluvial plains of Sind; and in the south the waters pass naturally into the Indus delta. East of the latter is the Great

Indian, or Thar, Desert, which is in turn bounded on the east by a hill system known as the Aravali Range, the northernmost extent of the Deccan plateau region. Beyond them is the hilly region of Rajasthan and the Malwa Plateau. To the south is the Kathiawar Peninsula, forming both geographically and culturally an extension of Rajasthan. All of these regions have a relatively denser population than the preceding group, but for topographical reasons they have tended to be somewhat isolated, at least during historical times.

East of the Punjab and Rajasthan, northern India develops into a series of belts running broadly west to east and following the line of the foothills of the Himalayan ranges in the north. The southern belt consists of a hilly, forested area broken by the numerous escarpments in close association with the Vindhya Range, including the Bhander, Rewa, and Kaimur plateaus. Between the hills of central India and the Himalayas lies the Ganges River valley proper, constituting an area of high-density population, moderate rainfall, and high agricultural productivity. Archaeology suggests that, from the beginning of the 1st millennium BCE, rice cultivation has played a large part in supporting this population. The Ganges valley divides into three major parts: to the west is the Ganges-Yamuna Doab (the land area that is formed by the confluence of the two rivers); east of the confluence lies the middle Ganges valley, in which population tends to increase and cultivation of rice predominates; and to the southeast lies the extensive delta of the combined Ganges and Brahmaputra rivers. The Brahmaputra flows from the northeast, rising from the Tibetan Himalayas and emerging from the mountains into the Assam valley, being bounded on the east by the Patkai Bum Range and the Naga Hills and on the south by the Mikir, Khasi, Jaintia, and Garo hills. There is plenty of evidence that influences reached India from the northeast in ancient times, even if they are less prominent than those that arrived from the northwest.

Along the Deccan plateau there is a gradual eastward declivity, which dispenses its major river systems—the Mahanadi, Godavari, Krishna, and Kaveri (Cauvery)—into the Bay of Bengal. Rising some

3,000 feet (1,000 metres) or more along the western edge of the Deccan, the escarpment known as the Western Ghats traps the moisture of winds from the Arabian Sea, most notably during the southwest monsoon, creating a tropical monsoon climate along the narrow western littoral and depriving the Deccan of significant precipitation. The absence of snowpack in the south Indian uplands makes the region dependent entirely on rainfall for its streamflow. The arrival of the southwest monsoon in June is thus a pivotal annual event in peninsular culture.

India from the Paleolithic Period to the decline of the Indus civilization

The earliest periods of Indian history are known only through reconstructions from archaeological evidence. Since the late 20th century, much new data has emerged, allowing a far fuller reconstruction than was formerly possible. This section will discuss five major periods: (1) the early prehistoric period (before the 8th millennium BCE), (2) the period of the prehistoric agriculturalists and pastoralists (approximately the 8th to the mid-4th millennium BCE), (3) the Early Indus, or Early Harappan, Period (so named for the excavated city of Harappa in eastern Pakistan), witnessing the emergence of the first cities in the Indus River system (c. 3500–2600 BCE), (4) the Indus, or Harappan, civilization (c. 2600–2000 BCE, or perhaps ending as late as 1750 BCE), and (5) the Post-Urban Period, which follows the Indus civilization and precedes the rise of cities in northern India during the second quarter of the 1st millennium BCE (c. 1750–750 BCE).

The materials available for a reconstruction of the history of India prior to the 3rd century BCE are almost entirely the products of archaeological research. Traditional and textual sources, transmitted orally for many centuries, are available from the closing centuries of the 2nd millennium BCE, but their use depends largely on the extent to which any passage can be dated or associated with archaeological evidence. For the rise of civilization in the Indus valley and for contemporary events in other parts of the subcontinent, the evidence of archaeology is still the principal source of information. Even when it becomes possible to read the short inscriptions of the Harappan seals, it is unlikely that they will provide much information to supplement other sources. In those circumstances it is necessary to approach the early history of India largely through the eyes of the archaeologists, and it will be wise to retain a balance between an objective assessment of archaeological data and its synthetic interpretation.

The early prehistoric period

In the mid-19th century, archaeologists in southern India identified hand axes comparable to those of Stone Age Europe. For nearly a century thereafter, evaluation of a burgeoning body of evidence consisted in the attempt to correlate Indian chronologies with the well-documented European and Mediterranean chronologies. As the vast majority of early finds were from surface sites, they long remained without precise dates or cultural contexts. More recently, however, the excavation of numerous cave and dune sites has yielded artifacts in association with organic material that can be dated using the carbon-14 method, and the techniques of thermoluminescent and paleomagnetic analysis now permit dating of pottery fragments and other inorganic materials. Research beginning in the late 20th century has focused on the unique environment of the subcontinent as the context for a cultural evolution analogous to, but not uniform with, that of other regions. Increasing understanding of plate tectonics, to cite one development, has greatly advanced this endeavour.

Most outlines of Indian prehistory have employed nomenclature once thought to reflect a worldwide sequence of human cultural evolution. The European concept of the Old Stone Age, or Paleolithic Period (comprising Lower, Middle, and Upper stages), remains useful with regard to South Asia in identifying levels of technology, apart from any universal time line. Similarly, what has been called the Indian Mesolithic Period (Middle Stone Age) corresponds in general typological terms to that of Europe. For the subsequent periods, the designations Neolithic Period (New Stone Age) and Chalcolithic Age (Copper-Stone Age) also are applied, but increasingly, as archaeology has yielded more-detailed cultural profiles for those periods, scholars have come to emphasize the subsistence bases of early societies—e.g., hunting and gathering, pastoralism, and agriculture. The terms Early Harappan and Harappan (from the site where remains of a major city of the Indus civilization were discovered in 1921) are used primarily in a chronological way but also loosely in a cultural sense, relating respectively to periods or cultures that preceded the appearance of city life in the Indus valley and to the Indus civilization itself.

X

Pre Mughal Dynasties

The table provides a chronological list of the dynasties that ruled in India before the Mughal Empire.

Pre-Mughal Indian dynasties

dynastylocationdates

NandaGanges River valleyc. 343–c. 321 BCE

MauryanIndia, barring the area south of Mysore (Karnataka)c. 321–185 BCE

Indo-Greeksnorthern India2nd century BCE

ShungaGanges River valley and parts of central Indiac. 185–c. 73 BCE

Satavahananorthern Deccanc. 100 BCE–c. 300 CE

Shakawestern Indiac. 100–c. 300 CE

Kushannorthern India and Central Asia2nd century BCE–3rd century CE

Guptanorthern Indiaearly 4th–late 6th century

Harshanorthern India606–647

PallavaTamil Naduearly 4th–late 9th century

Western Chalukyawestern and central Deccan543–757

Gurjara-Pratihara (I)western India and upper Ganges River valley6th–9th century

Eastern ChalukyaAndhra Pradeshc. 624–c. 1070

PalaBihar and Bengal8th century–12th century

Gurjara-Pratihara (II)western India and upper Ganges River valley8th–11th century

Rashtrakutawestern and central Deccanc. 755–975

CholaTamil Naduc. 850–1279

ChandelaBundelkhandearly 9th century–1082

CauhanRajasthan11th–12th century

Paramarawestern and central India10th century–1305

Later Western Chalukyawestern and central Deccanc. 975–c. 1189

Hoysalacentral and southern Deccanc. 1006–c. 1346

Yadavanorthern Deccan12th–14th century

PandyaTamil Nadu4th–14th century

Prime ministers of India

The table provides a chronological list of the prime ministers of India.

Prime ministers of India

namepartyterm

Jawaharlal NehruCongress1947-64

Lal Bahadur ShastriCongress1964-66

Indira GandhiCongress1966-77

Morarji DesaiJanata1977-79

Charan SinghJanata1979-80

Indira GandhiCongress (I)1980-84

Rajiv GandhiCongress (I)1984-89

V.P. SinghJanata Dal1989-90

Chandra ShekharJanata Dal (S)1990-91

P.V. Narasimha RaoCongress (I)1991-96

Atal Bihari VajpayeeBharatiya Janata1996

H.D. Deve GowdaJanata Dal1996-97

Inder K. GujralJanata Dal1997-98

Atal Bihari VajpayeeBharatiya Janata1998-2004

Manmohan SinghCongress2004-14

Narendra ModiBharatiya Janata2014-

Conclusion

This is not the end but couldn't write anymore will try to describe this country of gods India.

Printed by Libri Plureos GmbH in Hamburg,
Germany